When the Truth Hurts:
Lying to Be Kind

Bella DePaulo, Ph.D.

DoubleDoor Books

WHEN THE TRUTH HURTS may be purchased for educational, business, or sales promotional use. For information, contact the author or DoubleDoor Books.

DoubleDoor Books

DePaulo, Bella
    When the truth hurts: lying to be kind

ISBN-13: 978-1484120583
ISBN-10:   1484120582

FIRST EDITION: April 2013
DoubleDoor Books

Printed in the United States of America
10 9 8 7 6 5 4 3 2 1

About the Book

Most people value honesty. They want to tell the truth. They also value kindness. Sometimes, though, honesty and kindness collide. That happens when telling the truth would be hurtful, but being kind involves telling a lie. How do people negotiate this clash of noble intentions?

When the Truth Hurts: Lying to Be Kind is a book with two parts. **Part 1** is adapted from this chapter:

> DePaulo, Bella M., Morris, Wendy L., & Sternglanz, R. Weylin (2009). When the truth hurts: Deception in the name of kindness. In Anita L. Vangelisti (Ed.), *Feeling hurt in close relationships* (pp. 167-190). Cambridge: Cambridge University Press.

Thank-you, Wendy and Weylin, and thanks to Cambridge University Press for permission to reprint this work.

In **Part 2**, I have collected questions relevant to the topic of this book that I have been asked by various reporters over the years, and shared my answers.

I am grateful to the many reporters who have nudged me to think harder about the clash of noble intentions that occurs when honesty collides with kindness.

Part 1 was written for an academic audience, but any smart person will be able to understand it. Part 2 drops all insider jargon. It is not as detailed as Part 1, but I think it is more fun to read.

CONTENTS

When the Truth Hurts:
Deception in the Name of Kindness

Bella DePaulo, Wendy L. Morris, and R. Weylin Sternglanz

Everyone lies. It would be impossible to prove that definitively, but we believe it to be so. But we also believe that it is truth-telling, rather than deception, that is the human default position. People typically prefer to tell the truth. They want to be honest, they want to see themselves as honest, and they want other people to see them that way.

Ordinary humans – that is, the vast majority, who are not pathological liars – usually need a reason to lie. Lying, then, often grows out of a conflict. On the one side is the desire to be truthful, and on the other is some goal that cannot be attained (or cannot easily be attained) by telling the truth. Something has to give. If the sought-after prize is sufficiently shiny and bright, then often it is the truth that is left by the wayside.

Lying has a bad reputation. When we think of instances in which people set aside the truth to get what they want, often what we envision as the prize is something rather seedy or at least self-serving. Boatloads of money, for example. Or an ill-deserved promotion. Or 15 minutes of unearned fame. And in fact, people do lie for such reasons. But lies told for crass, materialistic, self-serving reasons are just one slice of the lie-telling pie, and not even a very big one at that.

Sometimes what truth telling bumps up against is not greed but graciousness. That, we think, is the most traveled intersection between lying and hurt feelings. People lie when they cannot both tell the truth, <u>and</u> be kind and gracious, at the same time. Something has to give, and what gives in these instances is usually the truth. In fact, we believe that in situations in which the truth would hurt, our inclination to avoid causing emotional pain – even just a tiny bit of it – is so overlearned that the usual default is overridden. That is, when hurt feelings are at stake, our first inclination is to lie.

In this chapter, we will examine the various types of lies people tell to spare the feelings of others. We will explore both the kind-hearted lies that people tell on a daily basis without much forethought or discomfort as well as the most serious lies people have ever told or been told. When people must choose between truthfulness and kindness, what factors will tip the scale more heavily in one direction or the other? This chapter will provide some answers to this question and also illustrate the tactics we use when we want to avoid hurting someone's feelings without telling an outright lie.

Lying in Everyday Life: Do Hurt Feelings Play a Part?

When we first set out to study the nature of lying in everyday life, there were only a few scattered studies of the phenomenon (e.g., Camden, Motley, & Wilson, 1984; Hample, 1980; Lippard, 1988; Metts, 1989; Turner, Edgley, & Olmstead, 1975) . Most were limited in some ways. For example, in some the

2

sample size was small. In others, participants described just one conversation or just one lie and could choose any conversation or lie they wished. In none of the studies did participants keep track of all of their social interactions (regardless of whether they had lied during those interactions). Doing so is important in that it provides an indication of the number of opportunities the participants had to tell their lies.

So in the studies we conducted (DePaulo, Kashy, Kirkendol, Wyer, & Epstein, 1996; DePaulo & Kashy, 1998; Kashy & DePaulo, 1996), participants kept a record of all of their social interactions (lasting ten minutes or more) and all of the lies they told during their interactions every day for a week. Participants described, in their own words, each of the lies they told and the reason for telling the lie. In one of the two studies, the participants were 77 college students, and in the other, they were a more demographically diverse group of 70 people from the community.

First, the basics. Apart from any consideration of hurt feelings, just how deceitful were our participants? The 77 college students told a total of 1,058 lies. That amounted to an average of two lies a day for each participant, or about one lie in every three social interactions. The 70 community members told a total of 477 lies. That was about one lie a day, or one lie in every five social interactions.

With regard to the content of the lies, people in both studies lied about the same sorts of things, and often in roughly similar proportions. For example, both the college students and the people from the community told many lies about their *achievements* and *knowledge*, often claiming greater accomplishments and more extensive learning than the facts of their lives could support. Participants in both studies lied often about their *actions, plans, and whereabouts*. They said that they had done things that they actually hadn't (such as giving to charity) and that they were planning to do things that they had no intention of ever doing (such as going to a boring social event). They made fanciful claims about being in a certain place at a certain time (home all night studying, or meeting with a client from work). Study participants lied about the *explanations and reasons* for their actions or inactions. One college student, for example, told his roommate this lie: "I didn't take out the garbage because I didn't know where to take it." In both studies, participants lied about *facts and possessions* – claiming, for example, to own an impressive vehicle or to have a father who is an ambassador.

In both studies, though, lies about achievements and knowledge; actions, plans, and whereabouts; explanations and reasons; and facts and possessions were all less plentiful than lies about *feelings*. In everyday life, people lie about their emotions, opinions, and appraisals more often than they lie about anything else. They claim to like people they dislike, and they pretend to agree when in fact they disagree. They compliment others on their ugly sweaters and hairstyles, and their misguided taste in music and food. They act impressed with a co-worker's holiday plans that they actually consider tacky. Sometimes they claim to dislike other people they actually do like. They also act emotionally unfazed, when in fact they are torn up inside.

When people lied about their feelings, they overwhelmingly overstated their positivity (or understated their negativity). For instance, they faked positive emotions they really did not feel, or hid their negative emotions. They exaggerated their liking for other people and places and things. They far more often faked agreement and interest than disagreement and disinterest. Feigning or exaggerating positive feelings, and hiding or understating negative feelings, is exactly what we would expect liars to do if they were telling at least some of their lies in order to avoid hurting another person's feelings.

We looked next at the referent of the lies – whether the lies referred to something about the liar, the target, another person, or an object or event. (Each lie could be sorted into as many referent categories as were relevant.) If participants were telling some of their lies about feelings to avoid hurting the target person's feelings, then feeling lies (compared to lies about other topics) should be especially likely to refer to the target of the lies. They were.

Finally, we examined the reasons our participants gave for telling their lies. Self-centered lies were motivated primarily by something the liars wanted for themselves, whether something psychological (such as making themselves look better or feel better) or more concrete (such as a promotion or a better deal on a purchase). Other-oriented lies were told to accomplish the same sorts of goals on behalf of someone else – for example, to make someone else look better or feel better, or to help them attain a more concrete goal. If the participants in the diary studies were telling lies to spare other people's feelings, then the lies they told about feelings should have been told more often for other-oriented reasons than for self-centered ones. Again, in both studies, they were.

Who Are the Targets of Self-Centered and Kind-Hearted Lies?

When we looked at all of the lies that our participants told, we found that most of them were self-centered. Only about 25% of lies were other-oriented (kind-hearted) lies. But the proportion of self-centered to other-oriented lies that people told depended importantly on the relationship they had with the target of their lies.

DePaulo and Kashy (1998) compared the ratio of self-centered to kind-hearted lies that were told to best friends, friends, acquaintances, and strangers. The disproportionate telling of self-centered lies occurred mostly to targets who were strangers or acquaintances. Both the college students and the community members told relatively more kind-hearted lies than self-centered ones when the targets of their lies were best friends or friends.

The desire to be kind and gracious, and to avoid causing pain, is likely to be most intense with the people we care about the most. Perhaps the desire to be honest is also most compelling with regard to the people to whom we feel closest. When the clash between kindness and truthfulness is complicated by closeness, what gives then?

In addition to looking at discrete relationship categories (such as friends and strangers), DePaulo and Kashy also did analyses that included all relationship partners (for example, parents, children, other relatives, spouse). Participants had recorded their closeness to each of their interaction partners on the same rating scale. Participants told relatively more kind-hearted than self-centered lies to the targets to whom they felt closer. Emotionally closer relationship partners should be just the people whose feelings matter most, and whose feelings liars would be most motivated to spare. That's what the results seemed to suggest.

How Often Are Hurt Feelings Implicated in the Telling of Everyday Lies?

Because these studies were not originally designed specifically to examine the role of hurt feelings in the telling of lies, we did not initially code anything so precise as the telling of lies in order to avoid hurting another person's feelings. We revisited the original descriptions of the 1535 lies (1058 from the college students and 477 from the community members), in the participants' own words, to see whether the participants framed the lies they told, or the reasons for telling their lies, in the language of hurt feelings. In 83 instances (5.4% of all lies), they did so unambiguously. As in the first example in Table 1,

Lie: *Said her hair looked great when it looked terrible.*
Reason: So I wouldn't hurt her feelings.

participants said they told their lies so as not to hurt the feelings of the other person. Another 20 gave reasons that seemed to amount to the same thing. As in the second example in Table 1,

Lie: *Told her I liked her new sweater. (Really thought it was ugly.)*
Reason: Didn't want her to feel bad.

they said they told their lies so the other person would not feel badly. Six more said they were concerned about the level of caring that would have been conveyed to the other person if they had told the truth rather than a lie. As in the third example,

Lie: *I said I didn't send a birthday card because I couldn't get to the store when actually I could have if I had really tried.*
Reason: I didn't want the person to think I didn't care about her birthday.

they lied to communicate more caring than they really did feel. Finally, in thirteen other instances, we inferred that participants were trying to avoid hurting the other person's feelings, though the participants did not say so directly (see the fourth example in Table 1).

8

Lie: *I lied and told her I wanted to see her more than I wanted to see my boyfriend.*
Reason: I didn't want her to feel like our relationship is decreasing in importance to me because of my boyfriend.

All told, then, 122 of the 1535 lies (7.9%) were in some way about hurt feelings.

In nearly all of the lies about hurt feelings, participants said they were trying to spare the feelings of the other person. But there were a few exceptions. In nine instances, participants lied to cover their own wounded feelings with a veneer of invulnerability (as in the fifth example).

Lie: *I told him I didn't care that he had a date.*
Reason: So I wouldn't appear vulnerable.

In two more instances, participants explicitly said they were trying to avoid getting hurt (see the sixth example).

Lie: *I said I wasn't hurt and that I wasn't ready to become involved with him.*
Reason: In order to protect myself from getting hurt or receiving his sympathy.

In another two examples, participants said that they were trying to spare both their own feelings and the other person's (see example seven).

Lie: *Pretended not to mind that we couldn't carry out our plans for the afternoon when actually I was irritated.*
Reason: Saw no reason to tell the truth, would only make us both feel bad.

We found just two examples in which participants were not trying to spare anyone's feelings. Instead, they seemed to be trying deliberately to hurt another person. (See example eight in Table 1.)

Lie: *Stated that I would like to plan a trip to Paris and Italy this summer. I know I can't plan a trip, since I can't afford a trip.*
Reason: It was my way of, once again, saying I don't need you to make me happy.

Of course, as in any self-report study, there is always the possibility that people may under-report socially undesirable behaviors – such as lying for the expressed purpose of hurting someone.

Table 1

What Counts as a Lie about Hurt Feelings? Eight Examples.

1.   **Lie:** *Said her hair looked great when it looked terrible.*
   Reason: So I wouldn't hurt her feelings.

2.   **Lie:** *Told her I liked her new sweater.*
   Reason: Didn't want her to feel bad.
   (Really thought it was ugly.)

3.   **Lie:** *I said I didn't send a birthday card because I couldn't get to the store when actually I could have if I had really tried.*
   Reason: I didn't want the person to think I didn't care about her birthday.

4.   **Lie:** *I lied and told her I wanted to see her more than I wanted to see my boyfriend.*
   Reason: I didn't want her to feel like our relationship is decreasing in importance to me because of my boyfriend.

5.   **Lie:** *I told him I didn't care that he had a date.*
   Reason: So I wouldn't appear vulnerable.

6.   **Lie:** *I said I wasn't hurt and that I wasn't ready to become involved with him.*
   Reason: In order to protect myself from getting hurt or receiving his sympathy.

11

7.   **Lie:** *Pretended not to mind that we couldn't*
       carry out our plans for the afternoon
       when actually I was irritated.
       Reason: Saw no reason to tell the truth, would only
       make us both feel bad.

8.   **Lie:** *Stated that I would like to plan a trip to Paris and*
       Italy this summer. I know I can't plan a trip, since I can't
       afford a trip.
       Reason: It was my way of, once again, saying
       I don't need you to make me happy.

Close Cousins to Lies About Hurt Feelings

We tried not to read too much into participants' descriptions of their lies or their reasons for telling their lies. We also refrained from stretching the hurt feelings category beyond what we perceived as its proper theoretical limits. The matter of discriminant validity, though, was not always straightforward.

In Table 2, we have listed the lies we regarded as close cousins of lies about hurt feelings. Ultimately, we did not count them in our tallies of hurt feelings lies, but we considered them. These close relatives of lies about hurt feelings included lies told to elicit sympathy, or to keep sympathy far away. Lies told to buoy another person's hopes, or to refrain from angering someone, are among the other examples.

Table 2

Examples of Close Cousins of Lies about Hurt Feelings

1.   **Lie:** *I said I had gained 5 points this weekend and I was fat.*
Reason: So they would respond to make me feel better.

2.   **Lie:** *Lie about my relationship with her brother.*
Reason: To make myself look nonchalant.

3.   **Lie:** *I said I didn't care about a car wreck.*
Reason: To appear nonchalant.

4.   **Lie:** *I told her I was not depressed and I really was.*
Reason: I didn't want her to feel sorry for me.

5.   **Lie:** *Told her I didn't feel any guilt over my mother's death.*
Reason: She was worried about me and to reassure myself.

6.   **Lie:** *Told Trona my nightmares were about different subject.*
Reason: My nightmares are about my Mother's death and I didn't want her to feel sorry for me.

7. **Lie:** *He was an old boyfriend and I told him I was glad he stopped going out.*
   Reason: Because I didn't want him to think I still liked him.

8. **Lie:** *I told Ruth that I though she had made the right decision about her boyfriend.*
   Reason: She was upset about her boyfriend and needed reassurance from me.

9. **Lie:** *Said I would like to see him over Thanksgiving.*
   Reason: To make him feel good since he was depressed.

10. **Lie:** *Deceived them about something that was going to happen in the future.*
    Reason: To make them worry.

11. **Lie:** *I told her I thought this guy really liked her.*
    Reason: I didn't want to destroy her hopes.

12. **Lie:** *I told her that her ex-boyfriend (my roommate) had not told me whether or not he still wanted to go out with her. (He does.)*
    Reason: I lied to protect my roommate – she can be a cold b*tch, but I like her.

13. **Lie:** *I told her I would call one of our friends because he was depressed.*
    Reason: To make myself feel better because I hadn't been keeping in touch.

15

14. **Lie:** *I told her I hadn't been home and wasn't going home until Thanksgiving.*
    Reason: I had gone home last weekend and I didn't want her to know it was because I didn't go and see her. If she found out she would get mad.

15. **Lie:** *I told her I was not depressed and really I was.*
    Reason: I didn't want her to feel sorry for me.

16. **Lie:** *She woke up late and I told her I didn't care if we were late to class.*
    Reason: So she wouldn't feel bad.

17. **Lie:** *She told me about a personal problem and I said that I understood why she felt the way she did when actually I didn't agree with her feelings at all.*
    Reason: She was really upset so I wanted her to feel better by thinking someone understood.

18. **Lie:** *I told her I love for her to stay with me and my family if she wanted to when I really wanted to be alone with them.*
    Reason: She was lonely and I didn't want her to have to stay in the dorm by herself.

19. **Lie:** *I said I didn't know who my stranger date was and thought it didn't really matter when really it does matter to me.*
    Reason: I don't want to seem too worried about liking this guy since it's just one date.

20.   **Lie:** *Said this guy liked her when he really hates her guts.*
        Reason: To get back at her for setting me up
        with a pig.

The Role of Hurt Feelings in Lying and Truth-Telling: Is It Mostly a Matter of Devalued Relationships?

Leary and his colleagues have proposed that at the heart of hurt feelings is "the sense that one's relationship is not sufficiently valued" (Leary, Springer, Negel, Ansell, & Evans, 1998, p. 1225). Relational devaluation, they explain, is "the perception that another individual does not regard his or her relationship with the person to be as important, close, or valuable as the person desires." Others have broadened or qualified the scope of the construct of hurt feelings, but because the Leary definition has been so influential, it is useful to start there and see how well it accounts for the experiences participants described in our studies of everyday lies.

When participants believed that they valued a relationship less than the other person did, they sometimes lied to spare the other person's feelings. Perhaps the prototypical version of this lie is the first example in Table 3.

> **Lie:** *Said I didn't know how I felt about him when I do.*
> **Reason:** I didn't want to hurt him.

One person is interested in pursuing a relationship, but the other is not. Rather than expressing disinterest clearly and directly, the uninterested party lies. In the second example in Table 3, the liar promises a friend and her mom to come back to visit, with no actual intention of so doing.

Lie: *Told her I would be back in a few weeks and that I'd stop by to see her and her mom.*
Reason: I didn't want to hurt her feelings.

Again, the relationship is less important to the liar than it is to the liar's friend, and the liar hides that hurtful truth with a lie.

The third and fourth examples in Table 3 are also clear instances of lies told to shield another person from the painful awareness of being excluded or unwanted. In the third, the liar conceals from another person the fact that a group of friends has been working on a project without him for weeks.

Lie: *I said that some friends and I just recently started a project when it had been going on for weeks.*
Reason: I thought he'd be hurt if he knew he'd been left out.

In the fourth, a liar who is glad to hear that her co-worker has found another job claims instead to feel sorry.

Lie: *I sounded sorry she found another job, but I actually was glad.*
Reason: Not to hurt her feelings.

Sometimes the liar is stuck in the role of the intermediary who knows that there is no way that Sally will go out with Harry, but tells Harry that she might. That was the case in the fifth example in Table 3.

> **Lie:** Told him my roommate might go out with him when I knew she wouldn't.
> **Reason:** I didn't want to hurt his feelings.

In still other instances, liars fake feelings not about the person they are deceiving, but someone else who is important to that person. Mary, for instance, might tell Harry that she likes Sally (even though she actually loathes her) because she knows that Harry likes her. These are lies told in the pursuit of affective balance: If someone I like (Harry) cares about someone I dislike (Sally), then I will claim to like Sally. That way, I presume, Harry's feelings will not be hurt.

> **Lie:** *Pretended to like Doug when actually I thought he was a real Geek!*
> **Reason:** Didn't want to hurt Kim's feelings.

Another type of lie, though, was even more commonplace than the Table 3 lies that quite directly spared other people from learning that a particular relationship was not as prized by the other person as it was by them. Superficially, they are lies that do not appear to be about a relationship at all. As in the first two examples of Table 1, liars are hiding their opinion of something belonging to or created by the other person, or something about that person's appearance, behavior, or skills. In the instances that seem relatively trivial, liars pretend to admire the other person's sweater, dress, earrings, hairstyle, ring, or Christmas

20

ornament. Or they claim to like the other person's homemade bread, muffins, or meatballs. Liars claim to be enjoying parties, lunches, and ballets, when in fact they are restless and bored. Other similar lies are about matters that may be a bit more significant. Liars offer the false reassurance that the other person seems to have lost weight, or looks just fine, or behaved reasonably and appropriately. They complement the other person's field hockey skills or art work, and act impressed by the person's enthusiastically-described holiday plans.

All of the examples we just delineated, in which the relationship-relevance is not immediately apparent, seem to fit under the category of shielding the other person from criticism. And in fact, in the Leary et al. (1998) research, participants said that they had their feelings hurt by criticism more than any other event (such as being betrayed, rejected, ignored, unappreciated, or teased). Leary et al. (1998) suggest two ways in which criticism may convey a devalued relationship. In their words, "First, criticism inherently indicates that the perpetrator holds some aspect of the victim in low regard. To the extent that the attribute being criticized is relevant to one's desirability as a friend, lover, employee, or acquaintance, the victim may infer that the perpetrator does not value the relationship as much as desired. [Also] the mere fact that the perpetrator has criticized them, often harshly, may suggest to the victim that the perpetrator does not value their relationship" (p. 1233).

Perhaps Leary and his colleagues are correct in suggesting that criticism of an aspect of another person is relationship-relevant, at least indirectly. In another set of examples we found, though, the relationship-relevance seems even less clear.

When people do better than others at a test or other performance, they sometimes understate their accomplishment. They claim that in doing so, they are sparing the feelings of those who did not do as well. For example, one participant was studying in the library when a classmate asked how he had done on the exam. He lied and said "lousy." Here's the reason he cited: "Although I did well, I realized she had not; I wanted to prevent hurting her feelings." Liars give up something in telling these kind-hearted lies – their legitimate claim to a job well-done.

Vangelisti and her colleagues (Vangelisti, Young, Carpenter-Theune, & Alexander, 2005) seemed to be describing a similar category of hurt feelings under the label "undermining of self-concept." Their participants said that their feelings were hurt when another person "made them doubt their competence or self-worth" (p. 449). Examples such as these, among others, were what led the researchers to suggest that the causes of hurt feelings needed to be expanded beyond just the devaluing of a relationship.

Table 3

Lies About the Valuing of Relationships: Six Examples.

1. **Lie:** *Said I didn't know how I felt about him when I do.*
   Reason: I didn't want to hurt hum.

2. **Lie:** *Told her I would be back in a few weeks and that I'd stop by to see her and her mom.*
   Reason: I didn't want to hurt her feelings.

3. **Lie:** *I said that some friends and I just recently started a project when it had been going on for weeks.*
   Reason: I thought he'd be hurt if he knew he'd been left out.

4. **Lie:** *I sounded sorry she found another job, but I was actually glad.*
   Reason: Not to hurt her feelings.

5. **Lie:** *Told him my roommate might go out with him when I knew she wouldn't.*
   Reason: I didn't want to hurt his feelings.

6. **Lie:** *Pretended to like Doug when actually I thought he was a real Geek!*
   Reason: Didn't want to hurt Kim's feelings.

Tiptoeing Around Other People's Feelings: How And When Is It Done?

In the diary studies of everyday lies, we relied on participants to tell us about their lies, the people to whom they told their lies, and their reasons for lying. By the participants' own accounts, they did indeed lie to avoid hurting other people's feelings. But our experimental hearts wanted to catch them in the act. We wanted to create the conditions that would cast participants in a clash between the desire to be honest and the wish to avoid hurting another person's feelings. The study we will describe (DePaulo & Bell, 1996) is the only one we know of in which the motivation to avoid hurting another person's feelings was experimentally manipulated.

We started by collecting a set of paintings that were created by students in art classes. The paintings ranged widely in quality and style. We were hoping that the participants we recruited for our studies would have strong feelings about the paintings, really liking some and truly detesting others. Fortunately, they did.

When the participant first showed up for the study, the experimenter explained that the study was designed to help art students learn more about how art is perceived by people who are not experts. At that point, though, no art student was present.

The participants spent time in a room set up like a gallery. They chose their two favorite and two least favorite paintings in the collection, and rated their degree of liking for each one. They also wrote, in their own words, what they liked and disliked about each of the paintings. They were assured, honestly, that the art student would never see what they had written about the paintings.

Theoretically, lies told to avoid hurt feelings should be about something personal. In the context of an art study, the artist who created the paintings might take another individual's opinions personally. Negative opinions, in particular, might hurt. The participants who disliked an artist's painting should be reluctant to say so to the artist. They should be sorely tempted to lie – especially since they knew that the art student would never see their descriptions of what they really did think of the paintings.

After the participants had committed their opinions of the paintings to writing, we introduced them to an art student. (The art student was actually a confederate. Three women alternated in that role.) Deeper into the study, the art student would point to one of the participant's least favorite paintings, and say, "I painted this one myself. What do you think of it?"

The question should make the participant squirm both because the participant really disliked the painting, and because the painting was the creation of the very person asking the question. If the painting were not the artist's own, then the participant should not be as tempted to lie. To test this, the artist also asked the participant about the other painting that the participant detested, while making it clear that the painting was some other artist's work.

The artist also asked the participant about the participant's two most favorite paintings. Again, she claimed that one was a painting of her own, and that the other was the work of some other artist. We expected very little lying in these conversations. Why hide your positive feelings about a painting, regardless of whether it is the creation of the artist in front of you or some other artist's work?

We could have left the study at that, and looked for participants to lie most often when discussing paintings they disliked that were the work of the artist with whom they were conversing face-to-face. But we wanted even more evidence that participants were lying in order to avoid hurting the artist's feelings. So in one condition, the *polite* condition, we specifically instructed the participants not to hurt the artist's feelings. They were told that it was okay to admit to things they did not like about the paintings, or to disagree with the artist, but that they should try to be nice about it. "This study is supposed to be a learning experience," they were told, "but we don't want any of [the artists] to end up feeling badly because of it." In the *no-instructions* condition, we gave participants no particular instructions.

Still, we were not quite finished. We thought that in both the polite condition and in the no-instructions condition, participants would be tempted to lie about the artist's paintings that they disliked. So in a third condition, we turned up the pressure to tell the truth. In this *honest* condition, participants were urged to tell the artist "truthfully what you liked and what you disliked about each painting." They were reminded that in order for the artists to learn what non-experts really do think about art work, the artists would need to hear unbiased descriptions of the work.

26

Once the instructions were completed, the participant was introduced to the art student. She then proceeded to interview the participant about each of the four paintings – the participant's two favorite paintings (one of which was the art student's own work) and the participant's two least favorite paintings (again, one of which was the work of the art student). Each time, the art student began with a general question ("What do you think of this painting?"), then asked more specifically about what the participant liked and disliked.

Rates of Clear Truth-Telling

We conducted this study to see whether people would tell outright lies in order to avoid hurting another person's feelings. We will get to the rates of lie-telling in the next section. First, though, as a comparison, we want to show how often our participants told the truth clearly and unambiguously.

What would a totally direct and honest answer sound like? In response to the artist's opening question – "What do you think of this painting?" – the participant could simply say "I like it" when s/he actually did like it, and "I dislike it" when s/he didn't. If only the truth mattered, it should make no difference whether the painting under discussion was the artist's own work or some other artist's creation. (In fact, the participants really did feel the same way about the paintings that were or were not the artist's own work. We learned that from their initial ratings of the paintings, before they knew anything about the artists.)

The top row of Table 4 shows what our data would have looked like, had the participants told simple and direct truths in every condition. One hundred percent would say explicitly that they disliked the paintings that they really did dislike, and the same 100 percent would say explicitly that they liked the paintings that they really did like. No one (zero percent) would say that they liked the painting they disliked, or that they disliked the painting they liked.

Let's look first at the condition in which it should have been easiest to tell the unvarnished truth – when the participants really did like the painting they were discussing. That's the third column of the table. When participants were urged to be honest, or when they were left to their own devices, they really did tell straightforward truths between 79 and 91 percent of the time. They liked these paintings, and that's exactly what they said. It did not much matter whether the paintings they liked were the artist's own work or some other artist's creation.

There was only one hint that participants may have been shying away from telling a simple truth when that truth should have been easy to tell. The participants instructed to be polite were the ones who showed a twinge of reluctance to say explicitly that they liked a painting they really did like. Their reluctance was evident when the painting they liked was the other artist's work: only 69% expressed unambiguous liking.

Now let's look at the more challenging condition, in which the participants actually detested the painting they were asked to discuss. (Those data are in the second column of Table 4.) Again, if they simply told the unvarnished truth, then 100% of them would have said that they disliked the paintings they truly did detest. A quick glance at that column shows that regardless of the condition they were in, participants never even got close to telling high rates of simple truths when the truth was hard to tell.

The pressure to run from the truth was most intense for the participants who were discussing paintings they abhorred that were the art student's own work, and who had been explicitly instructed to be polite and avoid hurting the artist's feelings. In that condition, only 22% of the participants straightforwardly told the artist that in fact, they disliked her painting. When left to their own devices, 40% of the participants admitted that they disliked the artist's own work. But even in the condition in which the participants were urged to be honest, only 62% of them owned up to disliking the painting created by the artist sitting right in front of them.

When the paintings that the participants detested were the work of another artist, it was a bit easier for them to say explicitly that they disliked those paintings. But even then, far fewer than 100% of them fessed up to their distaste. The participants who were instructed to be polite admitted to their disliking of the other artist's work only 47% of the time (compared to 22%, when the disliked painting was the artist's own work). In the no-instructions condition, the participants said they disliked the other artist's work 64% of the time (compared to 40% when it was the artist's own painting). Only in the condition in which participants were instructed to be honest did they own up to their disliking just as often when the painting was the artist's own as when it was the work of some other artist. Even then, the rates of explicit truth-telling were just 62% and 56% (not a significant difference).

Looking back at the middle two columns of Table 4, there is a pattern that is evident in every condition. Regardless of whether participants were told to be honest or polite or not given any particular instructions, and regardless of whether they were discussing the artist's own work or another artist's work, participants were always more willing to say explicitly that they liked a painting they really did like than to say that they disliked a painting they really did dislike.

Table 4

Percentage Who Were Honest or Dishonest in Reporting Whether They Liked the Painting

True feelings:	Dislikes Painting		Likes Painting	
Claim:	*"I like it"*	*"don't like it"*	*"I like it"*	*"don't like it"*
	(dishonest)	(honest)	(honest)	(dishonest)
Honest answer (*hypothetical*)	0	100	100	0
Instructed to be honest				
Other artist's work	9	56	81	3
Artist's own work	3	62	91	0
No instructions				
Other artist's work	0	64	83	0
Artist's own work	16	40	79	0
Instructed to be polite				
Other artist's work	3	47	69	0
Artist's own work	16	22	81	0

Rates of Outright Lying

Bald-faced liars are those who would say "I liked it" when asked about a painting they despised. The relevant results are in the first column of Table 4. Clearly, the rate of outright lying was very low. The highest it ever got was in the challenging condition in which the disliked painting was the artist's own work. Then, 16% of the participants who were instructed to be polite and avoid hurting the artist's feelings, and an identical 16% who were given no special instructions, told an outright lie. They said explicitly and unambiguously that they liked the painting they disliked. Except when participants were instructed to be honest, the rates of telling outright lies about the disliked paintings were even lower when the paintings were the work of another artist. (In the honest condition, the difference was not significant.)

Unsurprisingly, the rates of telling perverse lies were nearly zero. That is, when the participants really did like the painting they were discussing, they almost never said that they disliked it.

If They Are Not Lying and Not Telling the Truth, Then What Are They Doing?

Stonewalling. When the participants were in the difficult situation of discussing a painting they disliked, they rarely told an outright lie and said that they liked it (first column of Table 4). But they did not often tell the unvarnished truth, either (second column). So what were they doing? The unwillingness to offer any clear evaluation at all seemed to amount to *stonewalling*. When the going got tough, the participants simply stopped saying what they really did think – or at least they refrained from stating their opinions explicitly.

The participants were more likely to stonewall (refrain from saying explicitly that they disliked a painting or that they liked it) when they disliked the painting than when they liked it. They stonewalled most often when they were instructed to be polite and avoid hurting the artist's feelings, and least often when they were instructed to be honest or were given no special instructions.

Stonewalling may have been a useful technique for participants who were in trapped in a Catch-22 situation: They wanted to follow the instructions (be polite and avoid hurting the artist's feelings), and they wanted to be truthful. When they disliked the painting, these goals appear mutually exclusive; however, stonewalling may have provided participants with a way to avoid both rudeness and outright deception. Although there is always the danger that the artist may realize that stonewalling implies a lack of praise, at least participants can comfort themselves with the knowledge that they *tried* to avoid hurting the artist's feelings.

Praising by implication. A close look at Table 4 reveals a very clever strategy that the participants seemed to use when trying not to hurt the artist's feelings. More so than the participants who were instructed to be honest or who got no particular instructions, the participants who were told to be polite were stingy in their compliments of the <u>other</u> artist's work, even when they liked that work. When they liked a painting, the polite participants were more likely to say so explicitly when the painting was the artist's own work. At the same time, when they disliked a painting, they were less likely to say so explicitly when the painting was the artist's own work than when it was created by another artist. The participants were conveying, by implication, a positive evaluation of the artist's own work. In comparison to how they discussed the other artist's work, the polite participants flattered the artist sitting right there with them. Yet they did so without telling an outright lie.

Amassing misleading evidence. We also looked in great detail at how participants responded when they were asked specifically what they liked and disliked about each painting. We compared every aspect they mentioned during the discussion with the artist to the aspects they wrote down on the forms before they met the artist. When pressed to say what they disliked about each of the paintings, participants on the average generated two more disliked aspects than they had originally written down. When pressed to say what they liked, they generated more than three additional liked aspects. They were not even-handed about this. They came up with more new aspects that they disliked when discussing the other artist's work, and more new aspects that they liked when discussing the work of the artist in front of them. Participants in all three instructional conditions engaged in this strategy of amassing misleading evidence that flattered the artist's own work.

34

Does Affection Tilt the Scales Toward Kind-Hearted Lies or Hurtful Truths?

In the art study we just described, the participants were all strangers to the art student, and we did not nudge them one way or another with regard to their feelings of liking for her. In the next study (Bell & DePaulo, 1996), we deliberately tried to get half the participants to like the art student more than they may have on their own, and the others to dislike her. We did so by leading half of the participants to believe that they agreed with the art student on most important issues, and the other half to believe they disagreed with the art student on those issues. This attitude similarity technique has been a reliable way of influencing people's liking in past research, and it worked for us, too. The other difference from the previous study was that in this one, all of the participants were instructed to be polite and avoid hurting the art student's feelings.

Again, the most telling condition was the one in which the participants deeply disliked a painting that was created by the artist in front of them. To the usual clash between the desire to tell the truth (but then hurt the artist's feelings) and the desire to spare the artist's feelings (but then tell something other than the whole truth), we added the complication of the participant's liking for the artist. The key question was whether participant's affection for the art student would tilt the scales toward truth-telling or toward lying when the truth was hard to tell.

As we had surmised, it was the truth, rather than kindness, that was sacrificed when the participants liked the art student. More so than when they disliked the art student, the participants stonewalled when asked directly what they thought of the painting they hated that the art student had created herself. Only 12% offered an explicit evaluation. In contrast, 23% were willing to say exactly what they thought of the wretched painting when they disliked the artist who created it, even though that artist was sitting right in front of them.

The sly game of evaluation by implication was also played out more clearly when the participants liked the art student than when they disliked her. Participants who liked the art student were significantly more likely to tell her exactly what they thought of the other artist's work (compared to her own work) when they disliked it (35%, compared to 12%). When participants said explicitly that they disliked another artist's work, and they did not express their dislike directly when talking about the work of the artist in front of them, they offered the artist an opportunity to draw an inaccurate, but flattering, inference. The artist just might have thought that the participants disliked the other artist's work more than they disliked her own. And, who knows – the artist might have even assumed that the participants didn't dislike her own work at all.

In contrast, when the participants disliked the art student, there was little difference in their willingness to spell out their disliking for the paintings, regardless of whether the loathed art work was created by the disliked artist (23%) or some other artist (27%).

As in the first study, participants amassed misleading evidence regardless of whether they liked or disliked the art student. In both conditions, they generated more new aspects of the paintings that they liked than disliked. But again, they tended to tilt the new evidence in an even more positive direction when the artist was someone they liked.

It was not surprising that the participants were kinder to the artist they liked than to the artist they disliked. What is noteworthy is that they achieved that extra increment in kindness at the expense of the truth. The flip side is that the disliked artists received more honest appraisals of their work.

Are Serious Lies About Hurt Feelings, Too?

In the diary studies of everyday lies, most of the lies that the participants described were little lies. On the average, the participants described their lies as not very serious. They also said that they did not bother to plan most of their lies, and they did not worry much about the possibility of getting caught. They did feel a slight twinge of discomfort while they were telling their lies, and just afterwards, but even these discomfort ratings were below the mid-point of the scale.

The people who recorded their everyday lies were undoubtedly concerned, in some instances, with the feelings of the persons to whom they told their lies. But the lies they described were not typically of the gut-wrenching variety. Same for the lies told in the art studies – surely, the situation we created was disconcerting, but it was not terribly consequential.

Do hurt feelings have a place in the most serious lies in people's lives, or are they confined to the lighter domain of little lies? To find out, we conducted another pair of studies to examine serious lies more directly (DePaulo, Ansfield, Kirkendol, & Boden, 2004).

As in the everyday lies studies, we recruited two samples of participants – one group of college students, and another sample of people drawn from the community. Half of the lies described were the most serious lie the participant had ever told anyone. In these studies, though, we also included the target's perspective. The other half of the descriptions were of the most serious lie ever told to the participant.

As in the diary studies, we coded the content of the lies that participants told or were told. In contrast to the diary studies of lying in everyday life, in which lies about feelings were the most commonplace, in the serious lies studies, more lies were about affairs than about anything else (23% for the college students and 22% for the community members). Next in line were lies about misdeeds, such as stealing money or crashing the car (20% for the college students and 23% for the community members).

Lies about feelings were coded together with lies about personal facts. An example of a lie about feelings is a wedding vow that was made by a woman who did not really love the man she was marrying. An example of a lie about a personal fact was told by a woman who concealed from a friend that she had just had a miscarriage. Together, lies about personal facts and feelings accounted for 21% of the lies told by the college students and 16% of the lies told by the community members. Among the college students, no category of serious lies contents (other than affairs and misdeeds) was more commonplace. Among the community sample, there was one more frequent category – lies about money and jobs accounted for 21% of the lies.

Based on the transcripts of the participants' descriptions of their serious lies, we also coded the motives for the lies. The two most basic categories were the same as in the everyday lies studies – self-centered lies and other-oriented lies. The other-oriented lies were told to protect the target or another person from harm or from distressing information. Usually, the upsetting information was about the serious illness or impending death of a loved one. College students were more likely than the community members to say that the most serious lie ever told to them was told to protect them from distressing news. Typically, it was their parents who told the protective lies.

The protective lies were told to shield the targets from distress. Still, they do not fit our usual understanding of lies told to spare another person's feelings. The people who told those lies (often parents) surely were not devaluing their relationship with their children. In fact, it was probably the intensity of their concern for their children that made it so difficult to tell them news that would be so distressing. Yet, from reading the targets's accounts of these lies, we think that their feelings often were hurt – not by the information that was withheld, but by the fact that the bad news was kept from them. Participants seemed hurt that their parents regarded them as too emotionally vulnerable to hear the news at the same time as the adults. We did not design the study to test this interpretation directly, though, so it remains speculative.

We separated the self-centered lies into those told for reasons of personal advantage (such as avoiding punishment or attaining ill-deserved materials rewards) and those told for psychological reasons. Only a few serious lies (4%) were told for the expressed purpose of hurting the target person (rather than sparing that person from hurt). Some of the serious lies were told to protect the liars psychologically. Typically, though, the liars were ducking confrontation, embarrassment, or relationship conflict, rather than trying to protect themselves from getting their feelings hurt. Some of these self-protective lies involved promises that were never kept. The liar is asked for a favor – sometimes a big one, such as to lend money for a mortgage – and cannot seem to decline in person. The promise becomes a lie (or is seen as such by the target) when the commitment is never honored. The final category of psychological reasons for telling serious lies involved lies told for reasons of identity-management or self-presentation. For example, one woman told a man she was dating that she had some of her writings published in a prestigious magazine.

Because the serious lies studies included targets as well as tellers of serious lies, we were able to ask the targets directly the extent to which they felt hurt by the lies they were told. Targets' reports of acting hurt

40

upon discovering the lie were correlated with their reports of crying and of feeling depressed and tense. Feeling angry and acting defiantly were correlated with each other, and comprised a set of reactions that were distinct from the cluster that included hurt feelings. The hurt feelings reaction was also separate from three other reactions: acting relieved, acting forgiving, and feigning indifference.

The college students reported feeling most wounded by the lies that were told to protect them from distressing information. They felt the least hurt by lies told by people who were trying to impress them. Although the college students were pained by the lies that were told to protect them from emotional distress, the parents (and others) who told such lies seemed unaware of their impact. Not one of the participants describing the most serious lie they told to someone else mentioned a lie they told to protect a son or daughter from news of a death or serious illness.

Taking Stock

Scholars have pointed out that people value openness and honesty in their close personal relationships, and feel hurt when their partners do not honor these implicit relationship rules (e.g., Feeney, 2005). If the desire to be truthful never conflicted with other relationship expectations, such as kindness and loyalty, then the matter of honesty in relationships would be less complicated than it actually is. When one person has acted in a way that is not totally honorable (as all humans do now and then), an honest acknowledgment of that bad behavior – especially to a partner who expects so much more – can hurt. The temptation, then, is to lie (Millar & Tesser, 1988).

Sometimes people in relationships lie when they have done nothing wrong at all. They simply do not like something about the other person (maybe something as trivial as what the person is wearing) or do not agree with the person's judgment (about matters weighty or slight). Again, saying so can hurt, and so lying can seem preferable. At times, even exemplary behavior creates a risk of hurting the other person, as, for example, when one person in a relationship does particularly well at a task and the other does poorly. Once again, the dilemma can be resolved in favor of deceit, as when superior performers hide and deny their successes.

Who Tilts the Scales Toward Deceit And For Whom Are the Scales Tilted?

Based on our own research, and other reports in the literature, we believe that there are sex differences at the intersection of lying and hurt feelings, but the exact nature and account of those differences remain to be seen. Lippard (1988) reported that the women in her study were more likely than the men to say that they lied in order to protect another person's feelings. In our art studies, the women (more so than the men) conveyed even more liking for the paintings that were the art student's own work than for the other artist's work. (But because all of the artists were women, those results cannot be interpreted unambiguously.) In our everyday lies

42

studies, we found that there was something special about the lying that took place between women. When women were interacting with other women, the rate at which they told kind-hearted lies was similar to the rate at which they told self-centered lies. In every other type of dyad (men with men, or women with men), self-centered lies clearly outnumbered other-oriented ones. In a study of lying in initial getting-acquainted conversations, Tyler and Feldman (2004) found that men and women lied equally when they did not expect to meet again, but that women lied more when they thought that they would interact with their partner again in the future.

Under some circumstances, then, women may be more likely than men to tilt the scales toward deceit when hurt feelings are at stake. As for the people who seem especially likely to elicit kind lies, rather than hurtful truths, from other people, relationship closeness is important.

In our studies of the little lies of everyday life, we found that for best friends and friends, more so than for acquaintances and strangers, the desire to be kind trumped the motivation to be honest. People told more kind-hearted lies (relative to self-centered ones) to their best friends and other friends. In fact, they showed the same inclination with all of the people to whom they felt emotionally close. Lippard (1988) and Metts (1989) have reported similar findings.

In one of our art studies, we found that even when two people start out as total strangers, and one comes to like the other simply by virtue of learning that that the two are in agreement on a variety of issues far more often than they are in disagreement, there is a shifting of the sands in the tug-of-war between truthfulness and kindness. Again, it is kindness that tends to win.

Compared to people who do not feel particularly close to each other, people in close relationships are not only more likely to lie to protect their partner's feelings but they are also less likely to notice certain forms of dishonesty in their partners. We have found that when one friend attempts to conceal negative emotions, the other friend is less likely to detect those emotions when the friendship is a particularly close one than when it is less close (Sternglanz & DePaulo, 2004). It appears that we often do not see the nonverbal cues that people do not want us to see if doing so could potentially damage a relationship (DePaulo, Wetzel, Sternglanz, & Walker Wilson, 2003).

But Why?

In our studies of everyday lies, we asked our participants to rate the extent to which they were protecting themselves with their lies (i.e., they would have felt worse if they had told the truth) and the extent to which they were protecting the target of their lies (the target would have felt worse if the liar had instead told the truth). Participants generally said that they were protecting the other person with their lies more than they were protecting themselves. But telling lies, even for a supposedly good reason, is problematic, perhaps especially in close relationships.

Deception in relationships is contested territory. Hints of conflict emerge from people's claims about the motives for the lies. When Kaplar and Gordon (2004) asked participants to write two autobiographical narratives each, one from a time when they deceived a romantic partner, and the other from a time when they were deceived by a romantic partner, the reasons they proffered for the lies were not the same. As liars, they claimed that they told their lies to avoid hurting and upsetting their partner. But as targets, they were more inclined to claim that their partner had deliberately hurt them with their lie, and that the lie was not justified. Their results echoed our own findings from our study of serious lies that were not restricted to the domain of close relationships.

Claims that people lie to protect others rather than themselves are likely to elicit a predictable response among skeptical listeners – "sure, keep telling yourself that." It seems unlikely that liars have only the other person's interests at heart, even in the most defensible situations. Telling a painful truth is not just difficult for the person who hears it, but also for the person who tells it and then needs to deal with the reaction it creates in the target and the consequences that ensue. As Hrubes, Feldman, and Tyler (2004) have explained, regulation of the liar's own emotions is at the heart of the motivation for many lies.

It has become part of the conventional wisdom of our time that the cover up is worse than the lie. The implication is that bad behaviors, if owned up to, are never as bad for a relationship as the lies told to conceal them. There is not much rigorous research on this matter, but the results of the one relevant study we know of does not bode well for our received wisdom. McCornack and Levine (1990) asked people to describe a recent instance in which a relationship partner had lied to them. They also asked the participants to rate the importance of the matter that was concealed, and the importance of the lie itself. Then they looked at whether the relationship was still intact a month later. Whether the relationship survived depended more on the importance of the information that was hidden than on the importance to the target of the lie. When liars claim that they lied because they assumed the other person would be upset by the truth, sometimes their assumption was exactly right.

The Lure of Lying to Avoid Hurtfulness – And the Costs

In the course of everyday life, when anger and vengeance are not at the fore, people are remarkably reluctant to give voice to their negative feelings and opinions, or even to mention distressing news that they had no role in creating. A well-developed literature on the MUM effect (Tesser & Rosen, 1975) has shown that people are reluctant to convey bad news, and prefer to pass it along to a third party than to tell it to the person to whom it applies and who is most in need of knowing it. Even in situations in which conveying critical feedback is in the job description and that critical feedback could be useful to the persons receiving it, people are still reluctant to pass along the negative evaluation. Supervisors, for example, do not like telling their employees that their work needs improvement, and often put off doing so (Larson, 1989).

The favoring of kindness over truthfulness has its costs. People like to have others who care about their feelings and say just what they want to hear. But sometimes they also value the person who will tell it like it is. Pontari and Schlenker (2006) illustrated this with their studies of intermediaries, who were caught between a friend who wanted to make a good impression on a potential suitor, and the suitor whose preferences were not in line with the friend's actual characteristics. Sometimes the intermediary lied about the friend, making that person seem more compatible with the potential suitor. Those intermediaries were well liked. Other times, the intermediary was more honest. Those intermediaries were respected.

Another Answer to the Choice Between Kind Lies And Hurtful Truths: Neither

We started our exploration of the intersection of lying and hurt feelings by asking the question of whether the truth or kindness would prevail when the two were at odds. That framing, we discovered, was too simplistic. As Bavelas and her colleagues pointed out (Bavelas, Black, Chovil, & Mullett, 1990), there is at least one other alternative. When caught between a hurtful truth and a kind lie, people prefer to choose neither. Instead, they equivocate. They try not to answer directly the question that was asked, they try to avoid stating their own opinion, and they deliberately make their statements unclear. In our art studies, we also found some strategies for dealing with

47

the dilemma that did not involve outright lies. Our participants who did not want to say that they hated the painting they despised, but also did not want to say they liked it, amassed misleading evidence instead. They also stonewalled, and implied a positive appraisal that they did not really feel.

A similar situation arises in the context of dating. How do people respond when asked on a date by someone they have no interest in dating? Here, again, the conflict between honesty and kindness rears its head. In this potentially hurtful situation, Folkes (1982) found that people tend to avoid providing truthful explanations to potential suitors, particularly if the real reason for rejection is based upon stable physical or personality characteristics of the person about to be rejected. Instead, people cushion the blow by telling vulnerable suitors that they must decline the offer because of reasons that are impersonal ("it's not about you"), uncontrollable ("the circumstances make it impossible"), and unstable ("things could change in the future"). Similar to the tactic of amassing misleading evidence about paintings, these types of explanations are much less hurtful than a brutally honest rejection and they imply a more positive appraisal of the person than is actually felt.

The Bottom Line

Although lying is often considered a form of betrayal, it is frequently chosen as the lesser of two evils when the other option is hurting another person's feelings. Even parents and teachers who attempt to instill the value of honesty in children may urge children to commit lies of omission rather than hurt another person's feelings. Often the advice is stated in this familiar way: "If you don't have anything nice to say, don't say anything at all."

Honesty may well be an important foundation for any close relationship. Still, the research we have examined suggests that a certain degree of dishonesty in the service of sparing hurt feelings may have its place in close relationships. After all, even with those we care about the most, there may be times when we just don't have anything nice to say.

References

Bavelas, J. B., Black, A., Chovil, N., & Mullett, J. (1990). *Equivocal communication.* Newbury Park, CA: Sage.

Bell, K. L., & DePaulo, B. M. (1996). Liking and lying. *Basic and Applied Social Psychology, 18,* 243–266.

Camden, C., Motley, M. T., & Wilson, A. (1984). White lies in interpersonal communication: A taxonomy and preliminary investigation of social motivations. *Western Journal of Speech Communication, 48,* 309–325.

DePaulo, B. M., Ansfield, M. E., Kirkendol, S. E., & Boden, J. M. (2004). Serious Lies. *Basic and Applied Social Psychology, 26,* 147-167.

DePaulo, B. M., & Bell, K. L. (1996). Truth and investment: Lies are told to those who care. *Journal of Personality and Social Psychology, 71,* 703–716.

DePaulo, B. M., & Kashy, D. A. (1998). Everyday lies in close and casual relationships. *Journal of Personality and Social Psychology, 74,* 63-79.

DePaulo, B. M., Kashy, D. A., Kirkendol, S. E., Wyer, M. M., & Epstein, J. A. (1996). Lying in everyday life. *Journal of Personality and Social Psychology, 70,* 979–995.

DePaulo, B. M., Wetzel, C., Sternglanz, R. W., & Walker Wilson, M. J. (2003). Verbal and nonverbal dynamics of privacy, secrecy, and deceit. *Journal of Social Issues, 59,* 391-410.

Feeney, J. A. (2005). Hurt feelings in couple relationships: Exploring the role of attachment and perceptions of personal injury. *Personal Relationships, 12,* 253-71.

Folkes, V. S. (1982). Communicating the causes of social rejection. *Journal of Experimental Social Psychology, 18,* 235-252.

Hample, D. (1980). Purposes and effects of lying. *Southern Speech Communication Journal, 46,* 33–47.

Hrubes, D., Feldman, R. S., & Tyler, J. M. (2004). Emotion-focused deception: The role of deception in the regulation of emotion. In P. Philippot & R. S. Feldman, (Eds.), *The regulation of emotion* (pp. 227-249). Mahwah, NJ: Erlbaum.

Kaplar, M. E., & Gordon, A. K. (2004). The enigma of altruistic lying: Perspective differences in what motivates and justifies lie telling within romantic relationships. *Perssonal Relationships, 11,* 489-507.

Kashy, D. A., & DePaulo, B. M. (1996). Who lies? *Journal of Personality and Social Psychology*, *70*, 1037–1051.

Larson, J. R. Jr. (1989). The dynamic interplay between employees' feedback-seeking trategies and supervisors' delivery of performance feedback. *Academy of Management Review*, *14*, 408–422.

Leary, M. R., Springer, C., Negel, L., Ansell, E., & Evans, K. (1998). The causes, phenomenology, and consequences of hurt feelings. *Journal of Personality and Social Psychology*, *74*, 1225-1237.

Lippard, P. V. (1988). "Ask me no questions, I'll tell you no lies": Situational exigencies for interpersonal deception. *Western Journal of Speech Communication*, *52*, 91–103.

McCornack, S. A., & Levine, T. R. (1990). When lies are uncovered: Emotional and relational outcomes of discovered deception. *Communication Monographs*, *57*, 119-138.

Metts, S. (1989). An exploratory investigation of deception in close relationships. *Journal of Social and Personal Relationships*, *6*, 159–179.

Millar, K. U., & Tesser, A. (1988). Deceptive behavior in social relationships: A consequence of violated expectations. *Journal of Psychology*, *122*, 263–273.

Pontari, B. A., & Schlenker, B. R., (2006). Helping friends manage impressions: We like helpful liars but respect nonhelpful truth tellers. *Basic and Applied Social Psychology, 28,* 177-183.

Sternglanz, R. W., & DePaulo, B. M. (2004). Reading nonverbal cues to emotions: The advantages and liabilities of relationship closeness. *Journal of Nonverbal Behavior, 28,* 245-266.

Tesser, A., & Rosen, S. (1975). The reluctance to transmit bad news. In L.Berkowitz (Ed.), *Advances in experimental social psychology* (*Vol. 8,* pp. 193–232). New York: Aademic Press.

Turner, R. E., Edgley, C., & Olmstead, G. (1975). Informational control in conversations: Honesty is not always the best policy. *Kansas Journal of Sociology, 11,* 69–89.

Tyler, J. M., & Feldman, R. S. (2004). Truth, lies, and self-presentation: How gender and anticipated future interaction relate to deceptive behavior. *Journal of Applied Social Psychology, 34,* 2602-2615.

Vangelisti, A. L., Young, S. L., Carpenter-Theune, K. E., & Alexander, A. L. (2005). Why does it hurt?: The perceived causes of hurt feelings. *Communication Research, 32,* 443-477.

When Honesty and Kindness Collide:

Popular Questions about
the Clash of Noble Intentions

I
The Psychology of Little Lies

II
Sex Differences in Lying in Everyday Life

III
Lying in Relationships

I. The Psychology of Little Lies

What is your definition of a "white lie"?

I think of a white lie as a little lie that is not intended to hurt anyone, and may even be told to avoid hurting another person's feelings (as when we exclaim in joy about a gift that was exactly wrong, but well-intended).

Are white lies always harmless? Are there instances in which people shouldn't tell them?

There can be risks. For example, suppose you tell a woman that you like her outfit when it is really awful, and then she wears it to a job interview! Or suppose you get a reputation for being the person who always says something nice and is always protecting other people's feelings. That can be good, in a way. But you will never be the person others go to when they really do want an honest opinion.

What are the things people lie about the most, and why do you think these types of lie are so common?

In everyday life, people lie most often about their feelings and opinions. They pretend not to mind when a comment or suggestion is made that they don't like; they pretend to like people they really don't like, and to agree with people when they really don't agree at all. What's interesting about these examples is that they are not what we think about first when we think about lying. Usually, what comes to mind are crass, materialistic lies. People do tell those kinds of lies sometimes. But more often they are lying to make themselves look better or feel better, to make social interactions go more smoothly, and so forth – the rewards are more psychological than material.

If we all lie (some more, some less), why is the concept of truth so admired? Why do we think so highly of it?

We don't realize how often we lie. In the studies my colleagues and I did in which people kept diaries of all of their lies, we asked them at the end of the study if they thought they had lied more or less often than other people their age. On the average, people thought they lied less often than average, which of course is impossible! Not everyone can be more honest than the average person.

In people's minds, truthfulness is often equated with openness and trust. Those are all very positive qualities in the abstract. But in our real lives, all of those qualities do not always go together. For example, we think that the people we trust are honest with us. But sometimes it is the people we care about the most who want to spare our feelings. So, if what they really believed would make us feel badly, then they might not tell us the truth.

Why do we think it's OK to tell small lies to others but when it's the other way around, we hate the fact that other people lie to us? How do we excuse this hypocrisy?

I don't think we recognize the hypocrisy. First, when it comes to our own lies, we don't recognize how often we lie. Also, we rationalize a lot of our own lies. So, we think that if we told the lie for a good reason (for example, to avoid hurting someone else's feelings), then it doesn't count as a lie. But of course, it does.

With regard to the lies that other people tell us, we may not be totally aware of how we would really feel if we were told the truth all the time. We think we want to know the truth, but would we really want to know every time someone disagreed with us, or didn't like what we were wearing or serving for dinner, or didn't like our work, or just didn't like us? That's hard.

In the research my colleagues and I did, when we asked people to tell us about their own lies, they often described lies that were not all that terrible. But when we asked them to describe lies that other people had told to them, they described more hurtful lies.

II. *Sex Differences in Lying in Everyday Life*

How do men and women differ as liars?

In a pair of studies my colleagues and I conducted in the 1990s, two groups of people – college students and people from the community – agreed to keep track of all of their social interactions and all of the lies they told during those interactions. They kept these lie diaries every day for a week. The two groups were very different, demographically, but their ways of lying were quite similar.

We calculated each person's rate of lying – the number of lies they told per social interaction.

The most basic question we were able to answer about sex differences was this one: Who lies more often, men or women?

If you guessed women, you are wrong. If you guessed men, you are also wrong. **In the rate at which they tell lies in their everyday lives, men and women are equals.**

Where the real differences show up is in what the men and women are lying about and whom they are trying to fool.

Think about **two main reasons for lying**:

- **Self-centered** reasons: These are the lies that are all about you. You tell these lies to try to make yourself look better or feel better, or protect yourself from embarrassment or disapproval or conflict or from getting your feelings hurt.

- **Kind-hearted** reasons: These are the lies you tell to help or protect someone else. You tell these lies to make other people look better or feel better, or to protect them from embarrassment or disapproval or conflict or getting their feelings hurt.

People generally tell more self-centered lies than kind-hearted lies. Who tells especially more self-centered lies than kind-hearted lies? Here are your options:

- Men lying to men

- Men lying to women

- Women lying to men

- Women lying to women

The ratio of self-serving lies to altruistic lies is especially lopsided when men are talking to other

60

men. Men tell somewhere between three and nine times as many self-centered lies than kind-hearted lies when they are talking to other men.

In only one of the four combinations do people tell just as many kind-hearted lies as self-centered lies. Can you guess which?

It is the last one. When women are lying to other women, they do not tell any more self-centered lies than kind-hearted lies.

Bottom line:

When someone is lying about how fast they ran or how well they performed, it is probably a man talking to another man.

When you hear people saying things they don't mean such as:

- I know just how you feel
- You did the right thing
- You look terrific!
- This is so delicious

you are probably listening to two women. That doesn't mean that women do not value honesty when they are talking with other women. Maybe, though, they value loyalty and their friendship with one another even more. These are the kinds of lies that are intended to be friendly and supportive.

III. Lying in Relationships

Do Relationships Need Lies to Survive?

Save a relationship with a lie? Not a serious one.

A reporter who had read my book, <u>Behind the Door of Deceit: Understanding the Biggest Liars in Our Lives</u>, got in touch about an interview. She had a hunch, she said, that relationships need a dash of deceit to survive. When she said relationships, she meant romantic ones. I think that "relationship" has a much <u>bigger, broader meaning</u>, as does "love."

So taking the bigger meaning first, let me answer the reporter's question with an anecdote. Because I studied deception for so long, and have found in my work that lying (or, at least the telling of little lies) is ordinary rather than extraordinary, occasionally I get challenged. A conversation partner or student or someone in an audience at one of my talks will claim that they never lie. Even more interestingly, some will vow to spend the next several weeks not telling any lies at all. I never suggest or encourage this, but I do ask them to tell me about their experiences.

Only a few people have actually followed through with their personal experiments in honesty, but the result has been the same each time. They have to call it off after a few days, and go back and apologize. They say they are sorry to the person whose party invitation they declined with the honest response that the person's parties are always boring - or that the host him or herself is boring. They ask for forgiveness for saying to the friend who asked that she really does look like she gained weight. They try to make it up to the coworker whose contributions they described, in all honesty, as not up to par.

Is it sometimes more ethical to fib than fess up?

I draw a big line between little lies and big ones. Serious lies - the big time betrayals of trust - are probably never good for relationships of any kind. Little lies are often a different matter entirely. Sometimes people tell these lies not because they don't value honesty, but because telling the truth conflicts with something else they value, such as being compassionate or loyal or reassuring.

Romantic relationships are hotbeds for serous lies. Serious lies are often told by and to other close relationship partners, too, such as parents. For example, when parents hide a grim diagnosis of a grandparent's illness from an adolescent, sometimes that grandchild will still feel badly about the deception many years later. There is an intriguing exception, though, to the rule that the most serious lies are told by and to the people who are closest to us: In the 238 stories of serious lies that we collected, only 6 of them involved a best friend.

How prevalent is lying in romantic relationships?

It depends on whether we are talking about the little lies of everyday life or the big, serious lies. We have some data on the prevalence of little lies. In romantic relationships that are not married relationships, people lie in one out of every three conversations. With a spouse, they lie in one out of every 10 conversations. We don't know whether people become more honest as they become more serious about the relationship, or whether they are more honest from the outset with the person they will eventually marry.

It is different for serious lies. When people lie about something big - such as an affair, or about some other terrible thing they did, or just about anything else they consider serious - they are more likely to tell those lies to the people they care about the most. Our spouses and the other people we feel closest to are the ones who have the highest expectations for us. That means it is especially hard to tell them that you have fallen so short of those expectations.

Are all lies bad?

It might seem so in the abstract. But we live in the real world. We might value honesty and want to be honest, but we sometimes value other qualities at the same time, such as compassion or loyalty.

Sometimes, two noble goals come into conflict. If you tell the truth, you will be unkind, and if you say something kind, it will be a lie. Sometimes when people lie to the ones they love, it is because they are valuing something else more than honesty. Maybe they are trying to be loyal, or to avoid hurting the other person's feelings. Maybe they think that the other person isn't in a good enough place, emotionally, to hear a painful truth.

Liars sometimes claim to tell lies so as to spare the other person from pain. Sometimes they really mean it. But they can also be using that as an excuse to give themselves an out.

Why do people lie to their partners and what do they lie about?

Sometimes people tell what I call "kind-hearted lies." Those are the lies told to spare someone else's feelings or make them look better to others or feel better. Examples include: "I know just how you feel;" "you did the right thing;" "you look great." If you care about someone, you are more likely to tell them those kinds of lies.

Many of the other little lies of everyday life are told to make the liars look better or feel better or get what they want. Those are the self-serving lies. They can be told because the liars really are thinking only about themselves, but there's another reason, too. Sometimes liars claim to be smarter or kinder or more accomplished than they really are because they are trying to impress another person. So, they puff up their own image because they care so much about what the other person thinks of them. They want to create a good impression, but they are not sure whether their true self will be good enough. So they lie. Probably more of this kind of lying goes on when potential partners are first getting to know each other.

Serious lies are a whole other matter. When we asked people about the most serious lie they ever told to anyone, and the most serious lie anyone ever told to them, they described lies about many different things. But the most common were lies about affairs.

About the Author

Bella DePaulo (PhD, Harvard) is one of the leading scholars of the psychology of deceiving and detecting deceit. She has authored more than 100 scholarly publications. Her expertise on topics such as the psychology of deception and single life has been recognized in the *New York Times*, the *Washington Post*, *USA Today*, the *Wall Street Journal*, and many other major national and international newspapers. Her work has also been reported in magazines such as *Time*, *Newsweek*, *The Week*, *AAR P Magazine*, *Economist*, *Atlantic*, *More*, the *New York Times Magazine*, and the *New Yorker*. Her op-ed essays have appeared in publications such as the *New York Times*, the *Chronicle of Higher Education*, and *Forbes*. Dr. DePaulo has discussed her work on ABC, NBC, CBS, CNN, CNBC, PBS, the BBC, and the Discovery Channel. She has lectured nationally and internationally, addressing such diverse groups as medical professionals, forensic scientists, school teachers, criminal attorneys, physicists, judges, women's centers, and mental health practitioners.

Dr. DePaulo writes the "Living Single" blog for *Psychology Today*, and is also a contributor to the Huffington Post. She has been a Visiting Professor of Psychology at the University of California, Santa Barbara since the summer of 2000. Much more information about her background, her books, and her contact information can be found at her website, www.BellaDePaulo.com.

Other Books by Bella DePaulo

The Hows and Whys of Lies

Behind the Door of Deceit:
Understanding the Biggest Liars in Our Lives

The Lies We Tell and the Clues We Miss:
Professional Papers

Is Anyone Really Good at Detecting Lies?
Professional Papers
(with Charles F. Bond, Jr.)

The Psychology of Dexter

Singled Out:
How Singles Are Stereotyped, Stigmatized, and
Ignored, and Still Live Happily Ever After

Single with Attitude:
Not Your Typical Take on Health and Happiness, Love
and Money, Marriage and Friendship

Singlism:
What It Is, Why It Matters, and How to Stop It